AF541191

Kashi

Kashi

The Abode of Shiva

Written and photographed by

VIJAY RANA

RUPA

Published by
Rupa Publications India Pvt. Ltd 2024
7/16, Ansari Road, Daryaganj
New Delhi 110002

Sales centres:

Bengaluru Chennai
Hyderabad Jaipur Kathmandu
Kolkata Mumbai Prayagraj

Illustration credit: Sunil Kumar

P-ISBN: 978-93-90260-81-2
E-ISBN: 978-93-90260-88-1

First impression 2024

10 9 8 7 6 5 4 3 2 1

Printed in India

To the five generations of women in my life:
Sukh Devi, Shakuntala Devi, Renu, Aditi and Ameya

Contents

PART 2

RITUALS, RENOVATIONS AND REFLECTIONS

Morning aarti at Assi Ghat

गङ्गातरङ्गरमणीयजटाकलापं
गौरीनिरन्तरविभूषितवामभागम्।
नारायणप्रियमनङ्गमदापहारं
वाराणसीपुरपतिं भज विश्वनाथम्॥

Whose tresses are beautifully decorated with the stream of Ganga,
Whose left half is eternally adorned with the presence of Devi Gauri,
Who is dear to Narayana, the slayer of the pride of Ananga or Kamadeva,
Salutation to that Vishwanath, who is the Lord of the city of Varanasi.

ओम नमः शिवाय

Introduction

Panoramic view of the ghats of Ganga during evening

It is said to be 'older than history and tradition, older than legend and looks twice as old as all of them put together'. In these simple yet eloquent words, Mark Twain, the American writer, was able to capture the essence of one of the oldest cities in the history of human civilization. Being at the heart of Hinduism's spiritual story, it has witnessed a myriad of celestial and earthly performances that have unfolded here.

Kashi, popularly known as Banaras or Varanasi, is said to be blessed by the supreme god and his consort. Believed to be the home of Parvati and Shiva, the city on the banks of the mighty river Ganga has secured a revered position in Hinduism. For centuries, it has attended to the needs of Hindu worshippers. Gods and gurus, sages and saints, the greatest of all have come to Kashi to find what they couldn't find elsewhere. Whether it was Adi Shankara from Kerala, Guru Nanak from Punjab, Mirabai from Rajasthan or Chaitanya Mahaprabhu from Bengal, no spiritual quest was complete without a pilgrimage to Kashi. Home to some of India's most enlightened minds, such as the fifteenth-century Bhakti saint and poet Kabir, the remarkable tenacity of India's Hindu civilization has surprised many observers and visitors. The city has welcomed and enriched the experiences of many, including some of the Greek historians in the first millennium BC, Al-Biruni in 1707, Mark Twain (who visited India at the end of the nineteenth century), Gautam Buddha, Swami Dayanand Saraswati (founder of the Arya Samaj), Sri Ramakrishna Paramahamsa and Swami Vivekananda, to name a few. To this day, Kashi enjoys the admiration and reverence of scholars, travellers, storytellers and worshippers.

At the core of this city, which continues to find pertinence in the contemporary world, lies the soul of the city, the abode of the Lord of the World, the revered temple of Kashi Vishwanath. According to the Bhagavad Gita, the soul remains indestructible, and hence the temple of Kashi Vishwanath stands imperishable

The golden spire of the Vishwanath Temple before renovation

in the heart of the city. Despite attempts of destruction, the temple has only risen time and again, each time with greater splendour.

Like other Hindu temples, Kashi Vishwanath presents a magnificent synthesis of spirituality, imagination and art. Ancient Hindus possessed the creative bent to build some of these fantastic temples, imagine beautiful idols of gods and devise vibrant devotional rituals. I always dreamt of somehow retaining a visual memory of these splendid sites. It seemed an impossible dream because most prominent Hindu temples had high security and massive crowds.

In addition to the hurdles of population, sadly, photography is banned inside most major Hindu temples across India. This prohibition has been particularly tightened in recent decades due to security concerns and crowd management. It is indeed ironic that a religion like Hinduism, which has thrived on idol worship and has produced many sculptural and architectural wonders, is now, in the twenty-first century, trying to prevent further dissemination of its artistic heritage.

It is not just about the photo documentation of our temple buildings, we are also missing out on one of the most fundamental aspects of our religious tradition. We have never tried to preserve a visual memory of the ritualistic practices performed inside these temples. As this book demonstrates, these rituals can be elaborate, exquisite and often awe-inspiring. They show us the depth and intensity of faith. What is even more interesting is the profound reason and story that lay behind each and every aspect of Kashi Vishwanath and the essence of the most sacred city for followers of Hinduism. The idea was to take these stories and bring them to the fore. The beginning of this long journey started back in 2017.

In February 2017, I began filming across Varanasi for my documentary *Banaras – The Story of India's Sacred City*. My friends in the city warned me that filming inside the Kashi Vishwanath Temple would be impossible. Despite these warnings, I firmly believed that visual documentation of the City of Shiva was bound to remain incomplete without filming and photographing the temple.

Luckily, the Kashi Vishwanath Temple administrator was convinced by my arguments. During my third visit to Varanasi in June 2018, I was able to persuade the temple administration to allow me to film inside the temple, including the sanctum sanctorum.

Armed with official permission, when I arrived at the temple gates, our team was thoroughly searched, and a bomb-disposal

Vishwanath Linga, covered in Shiva's favourite bael leaves and blue Aparajita flowers. One of the leaves stood like a serpent wrapped around Shiva's head.

squad examined our equipment. The temple was virtually squeezed into a corner of the Gyan Vapi Mosque. The space was so narrow that we could not capture the entire temple in one wide-angle shot. Filming inside the sanctum was a massive challenge. Holding a steady camera amidst devotees jostling for a momentary glimpse of Baba Vishwanath required considerable physical strength. Ignoring the crushing melee, I gathered the last drop of my energy, took a deep breath and continued shooting the black stone Linga of Vishwanath, covered with green *bilva patra* (bael leaves). When the devotees poured the sacred Ganga water over the Linga, a marigold flower majestically fell over it. In an exciting shot, I captured a bael leaf standing next to the Linga, resembling a snake wrapped around the neck of Lord Shiva.

After returning to London, I produced a six-minute film narrating the story of the Kashi Vishwanath Temple and its cramped and neglected surroundings. It was screened during Prime Minister (PM) Narendra Modi's programme at Banaras Hindu University (BHU) in September 2018. In 2019, owing to his constituency, PM Modi unveiled his ambitious plan to renovate the Kashi Vishwanath Temple. Costing ₹339 crore, the project aimed to create a spacious pathway connecting the temple to the sacred river Ganga, enhancing accessibility and fostering a sense of spiritual unity with the holy river among devotees. The grand plan involved acquiring and demolishing over 400 properties that had encroached upon some of the ancient temples in the area. This arduous task marked a turning point in the temple's history. With the removal of many unauthorized properties, the Kashi Vishwanath Temple emerged from the shadows of the haphazard developments around it. As per the latest December 2023 reports, Kashi Vishwanath has seen a record footfall of 12.9 crore devotees in the last two years.[1]

The rejuvenation of the holy site and, with it, the sacred city presents us with a unique opportunity to dig into its history and capture the essence of the city in its entirety. Taking a mixed approach, this captivating project documents the history and spirituality of Kashi by bringing together stories from ancient texts and merging them with the journey I undertook over the years. Through this, I hope to present to you, the reader, some of the most essential and intriguing stories behind the accepted beliefs, daily rituals and devotional practices of the city and its temple.

This book serves as a testament to the enduring spirit of Shri Kashi Vishwanath. It is a chronicle of a temple reborn, a symbol of India's rich spiritual heritage and a beacon of hope for future generations. The abiding spirit of Kashi cannot be experienced unless one visits the temple of Kashi Vishwanath. With the hope of drawing and inspiring people, I present to you an ode, a celebration of the city that is Shiva's abode.

Vijay Rana
London, 1 January 2024

Part 1

ANANDAKANANA KASHI: SHIVA AND PARVATI'S GARDEN OF BLISS

Pushp shringar (floral decoration) of the Holy Lord

1

Shiva and Shakti

The Creation of Purusha and Prakriti

Ardhanarishwar: The essential unity of Shiva and Shakti or Purusha and Prakriti

त्रयीमयेऽस्मिंस्त्रयमेव सारं ।।
विश्वेशलिङ्गं मणिकर्णिकाम्बु
काशीपुरी सत्यमिदं त्रिसत्यम् ।।

'In this world illuminated by the knowledge of three Vedas, only three things are essential: Vishweshwara Linga, the water of Manikarnika and the city of Kashi. This is the Truth, the threefold Truth.'

SKANDA PURANA, 'KASHI KHANDA', CH. 99, VERSE 61

Kashi is known by many names. There is an interesting legend attached to the auspicious names the holy abode is known by.

As the story goes, once the revered sage Agastya asked Lord Skanda, the son of Shiva and the narrator of Skanda Purana, about how Kashi came to be known as Avimukta and Anandavana, and how it acquired the reputation of being the holiest place on earth.

Pleased with these questions, Skanda told Agastya that the mother of the universe, Shakti, too, had once raised these questions with Mahadeva.

The omniscient Lord explained that once upon a time, all living beings had perished during *Mahapralaya* (the Great Dissolution). Even the sun, moon, stars and planets had disappeared. Darkness had spread in all directions. The fire and the wind had come to a standstill, and the sensations of sound, touch and smell had become extinct. It was the time when nothing existed, except the Supreme Absolute, also known as the *Sat* or *Brahman*. It was incomprehensible, inexpressible and infinite. It was only later that the yogis could perceive it as the truth, consciousness and ultimate bliss. It was *nirvikalpa* (without alternative) and *nirarambha* (without beginning). It was *nirmaya* (without worldly distractions) and *nirupadrava* (without troubles).[1]

Devotees singing the praise of Baba Vishwanath

While suffering from loneliness, the Supreme Being had a desire for creation. Therefore, he developed a glorious form. This form was endowed with all the consciousness and knowledge. It was an object of universal veneration and had the power to create a perfect world. It was pure and divine.

Shiva told Shakti that after creating that form, the Supreme Being vanished, leaving behind his newly created form, the Purusha. The learned sages knew the true nature of the new form and began calling him *Ishwara*.

Shiva said to Shakti, 'Simultaneously, this holy spot was created by me, the primordial purusha...in the company of you, the Shakti.'[2] Meanwhile, continuing his story, Skanda, the narrator of Skanda Purana, told sage Agastya that this holy spot is never left by Shiva and Shakti. It extends to five *krosas* (one krosa is equal to 3 km). It was created from the soles of Shiva's and Shakti's own feet. They never leave that holy place, even at the time of the great annihilation. Hence, it is Avimukta.'[3]

Sage Agastya asked Skanda about Shiva's divine assembly in Kashi. Skanda replied this assembly had been called by Shiva. He sat majestically, facing the east. His consort, Goddess Shakti, sat beside him, with Brahma settled

According to 'Bilvashtakam', composed by Adi Shankara, an offering of a cluster of three leaves to Shiva represents the three tamas. It also reminds us of the three eyes of Shiva and his trident. The root is Brahma, the middle is Vishnu and the top is Shiva.

Daybreak at the ghats of the
sin-cleansing Ganga

The merging of Shiva into Vishweshwara Linga in the presence of Brahma, Vishnu and other devas

on his right and Vishnu on his left. The Lord of Heaven, Indra, stood close, fanning him, and the devas and sages huddled around him. At the same time, Shiva's attendant Ganas stood in reverence, some with uplifted arms and others with joined palms. Addressing the assembly, Lord Shiva said: 'The Linga of Vishweshwara has the most extraordinary splendour. This alone is my immobile form that accords *siddhi* (the highest perfection) to my devotees.'[4]

'O Devas, I stay in this Anandakanana, Varanasi, as I happily bless all the devotees forever. There is no doubt that I remain in all the Lingas, but this is the greatest of my forms. Therefore, if a devotee faithfully sees this Linga of Vishweshwara with an untainted vision, it is as good as he has seen me. O Devas, listen along with the sages; if one hears the glory of Vishweshwara Linga, all his sins accumulated in three births will perish instantly.'[5]

'With my raised hands, I affirm again and again that in this world illuminated with the knowledge of Vedas, only three things are essential: Vishweshwara Linga, the water of Manikarnika and the city of Kashi. This is the Truth, the threefold Truth.'[6]

Then, the Lord of the Universe got up along with his consort Shakti and merged into the Vishweshara Linga. Devas and Ganas stood in reverence and uttered: 'Be victorious, be victorious...'[7]

Ghats of Ganga adorned with street art of Shiva and sages

A starving Shiva begging for food from Annapurna, the mother goddess of Kashi

2

Annapurna

The Life-Giving Mother of Kashi

Idol of Annapurna inside the Kashi Vishwanath Temple

अन्नपूर्णे सदापूर्णे शङ्करप्राणवल्लभे ।
ज्ञानवैराग्यसिध्यर्थं भिक्षां देहि च पार्वति ।।
माता च पार्वती देवी पिता देवो महेश्वरः ।
बान्धवाः शिवभक्ताश्च स्वदेशो भुवनत्रयम् ।।

'Oh! Mother Annapurna! You are always full; you are the life force of Shankara. Give me the alms of your grace to let me attain knowledge and renunciation. My mother is Goddess Parvati. My father is Lord Maheshwara. The devotees of Lord Shiva are my brothers, and the entire universe is my homeland.'

'ANNAPURNA STOTRAM', ADI SHANKARA, VERSE 11–12

The primordial union of Shiva and Shakti holds the equilibrium of this universe. Nowhere is this complementarity of the Purusha and Prakriti better expressed than in the story of Annapurna. In Kashi, the mother goddess Shakti is also known as Annapurna Bhavani, the female power behind Bhava, the Supreme Being.

Adi Shankara, who lived in the eighth century, described Annapurna as *Kashipuradhishwari*, the presiding goddess of Kashi. As the gracious mother of the three worlds, she sustains life by providing plentiful food. If Shiva is the ruler of Kashi, Annapurna is the mother goddess, feeding and nurturing her children and ensuring vital energy, essential life and material comforts.

There is a widespread belief that when Shiva and Shakti came to stay in Kashi, they made a mutual agreement that as long as a person was alive, the latter would sustain life and provide plentiful food. When the person would die, Shiva would grant them *moksha* (liberation from the cycle of life and death).

Several stories of Annapurna can be found in ancient texts, but the most popular one goes as follows. Once, Shiva and Parvati had an argument about the nature of human existence. The great ascetic Shiva believed that all material things of human interest were *maya* (illusion). He adamantly insisted that even food was maya. Parvati, the mother of the world and the protector of material well-being, disagreed. She pleaded with Shiva to have a balanced view. But Shiva stood firm.

A local boy dressed up as Shiva, trying to make a livelihood

His refusal to accept angered Parvati. She thought that Shiva was belittling her role as the governess of the material world. The feud between the divine couple escalated, and she resolved to demonstrate the importance of her stance. So, she left this universe. As soon as she left, all material things vanished. Time came to a standstill. Nothing grew on earth, and soon there was a severe famine. The scarcity of food and water brought untold suffering to the inhabitants of the universe. Even Shiva and the heaven-dwelling devas began to suffer from terrible hunger. They ran around searching for food.

Meanwhile, they learned that in the sacred city of Kashi, a kitchen still served food to the people. Craving for food and comfort, Shiva arrived in Kashi. To his amazement, he found Parvati serving *anna* (food) to the residents of Kashi. Holding a food bowl in her hands, the mother of plenteous food was busy offering grains to people. She had decided to return to her beloved Kashi because, owing to her vow and being a woman of her word, she could not bear the sight of people suffering.

To her great dismay, she saw a familiar face in the crowd. Holding a begging bowl, she saw a starving Shiva standing before her, pleading for food. She knew that Shiva had realized his mistake and was prepared to admit that existence depended on material needs, which was described by the learned sages as maya. Standing by her promise and letting go of the ignorant argument, she offered food to the hungry Shiva.

This story has and continues to resonate with Hindus, and so, a pilgrim's visit to Kashi remains incomplete without the ritual worship of the goddess Annapurna.[1] The devotees of Annapurna recite her thousand names. Some chant her 108 names, while others sit down in the temple to read the popular 'Annapurna Vrat Katha'. The story conveys a powerful message to the devotees that there is no father like Vishweshwara, the destroyer of rebirth, and no mother like Bhavani, the giver of plenteous food. This is the essence of Adi Shankar's 'Annapurna Stotram', which is regularly recited in many Hindu homes.

In Varanasi, the temple of Annapurna stands a few yards away from the current Vishwanath Temple. It was constructed in 1729 by the Maratha leader Peshwa Bajirao. There is also a life-size metal idol of Annapurna inside the Kashi Vishwanath Temple. This idol was installed in the temple in January 1977 by the Shankaracharya of Sringeri.[2]

A new chapter in the history of Annapurna was added in November 2021, when the Government of India managed to bring back from Canada an idol of Annapurna stolen more than a century ago.[3]

Free food being served outside Khichdi Baba Temple

In 1913, Norman MacKenzie, a Canadian art collector, had made a visit to Varanasi. An idol had captured his attention and he had managed to charm one of the temple attendants to part away with it. The idol had changed hands and countries, and it sat in a Canadian university museum for over a century. Until one day, Divya Mehra, a Canadian artist of Indian origin, noticed it. She found that the 17.30-cm idol was incorrectly labelled as Lord Vishnu. Mehra alerted the gallery authorities to the feminine characteristics and the graceful adornment like earrings and a necklace. A subsequent examination by a British expert confirmed the identity of this artefact. It was, in fact, an idol of the goddess Annapurna.

The stolen statue of Annapurna, brought back from Canada in 2021

It was duly returned to its rightful place, Varanasi. The people of the city came out in multitudes to welcome the presiding goddess of Kashi. Yogi Adityanath, the chief minister of Uttar Pradesh, performed *prana-pratishtha* (an elaborate deification ceremony). This ritual endowed the idol with divine status and a sacred object of worship. Today, this idol of Annapurna resides alongside the older idol of Annapurna within the holy precincts of the Kashi Vishwanath Temple.

Other than its religious significance, what is fascinating about Kashi is its undying spirit for cultural continuity. Even in the twenty-first century, the tradition of giving free food to the needy, started by Annapurna, is continuing in Kashi in a street-side temple, known as Khichdi Baba Temple, near Dashashwamedha Ghat. It is said to have been started by a local saint, Shankar Swami, more than a hundred years ago. Though little is known about him, he came to be known as Khichdi Baba. The temple serves freshly cooked khichdi to more than a thousand people every day. The temple is an impressive reminder of the spirit of Annapurna.

A young girl dressed as Goddess Parvati, trying to earn a livelihood

Idols of Vishnu and Virupakshi Gauri inside the Vishwanath Temple

Ishan Rudra digging up Gyan Vapi or the wisdom well

3

Gyan Vapi

Ishan Rudra Digs the Wisdom Well

Worshippers paying obeisance at Gyan Vapi

ज्ञानरूपोऽहमेवात्र द्रवमूर्तिम्विधाय च ।
जाड्यविध्वंसनं कुर्यां कुर्यां ज्ञानोपदेशनम् ।।

*'"I myself, in the form of Jnana, having assumed the liquid form,
shall destroy Jadya, the ignorance and impart knowledge," said Vishweshwara.'*

SKANDA PURANA, 'KASHI KHANDA', CH. 33, VERSE 50

Inside the premises of the Kashi Vishwanath Temple lies one of Varanasi's most sacred spots, the Gyan Vapi or the wisdom well. It is located inside a pink-stone arcade next to the main temple. The well is approximately 10 ft in diameter and has no water because it has now been covered with concrete. Before the well dried up, pilgrims used to begin their Kashi *parikrama* (circumambulation) after sipping its holy water.

As the story goes, in the primordial age of Satya Yuga, when few people lived on this earth, Ishan, who was identical to Rudra, one of the forms of Shiva, came wandering to the glorious Kashi. It was a time when clouds did not rain, oceans remained empty, and rivers like Ganga did not flow on this earth.

When the massive-bodied and matted-haired Ishan arrived at this holy place, he saw the glorious Linga of Light, the Jyotirlinga. This prodigious Linga had risen during the fierce battle between Vishnu and Brahma because both claimed to be greater than the other. Later, the gods and sages worshipped this Jyotirlinga. Siddhas and yogis venerated it. *Gandharvas*, a group of heavenly singers and musicians, sang its praise. *Apsaras*, the celestial damsels, joyously danced around it.[1] Moreover, the Jyotirlinga was decorated with garlands of colourful flowers three times a day, a practice that continues till date.

Ishan was incredibly impressed and thought of bathing this great Linga in cool water. So, to the south of the Vishweshwara Linga, he speedily dug up a bottomless pit with his trident and did not stop until gigantic columns of water burst out of the earth.

The water of the pit that Ishan had dug carried the bluish tinge of the sky and was cold like snow. Its brightness equalled the moonlight. Furthermore, in purity and holiness, it matched the name of Shiva Shambu. This water had the sweetness of divine nectar, the smoothness of the limbs of a cow and the splendour of the intellect of a sinless person. It had life-sustaining and

The 40-pillar colonnade of Gyan Vapi, built in 1828 by Rani Baiza Bai, widow of Raja Daulat Rao Scindia of Gwalior

knowledge-imparting powers. Ishan was delighted. He filled pitchers with this holy water and bathed the Linga a thousand times. Ishan's endeavour brought more happiness to Vishweshwara, and the Holy Lord was thrilled. He appeared on the scene and told Ishan, 'I am pleased with your great rite, never before performed by anyone else. Ask me for a boon. Today, I will give you anything that you want.'

Ishan replied, 'O Devesh, Lord of the Devas, if you want to grant me a boon, let this extraordinary site be a holy Tirtha named after you.'

Vishweshwara said, 'Surely, this Tirtha would be greater than all the Tirthas of the three worlds. Because the learned men say Shiva means knowledge and wisdom, and this knowledge has taken a liquid form, therefore, this Tirtha would be known as Gyanoda. Anyone who touches or sips this sacred water would eliminate all sins and have benefits equal to performing the *Ashvamedha Yagna* (horse sacrifice).'

A makeshift idol of Shiva inside Gyan Vapi during Rangbhari Ekadashi

Vishweshwara continued, 'This would henceforth be called Shiva Tirtha, Gyana Tirtha and Taraka Tirtha—the sacred place of Shiva, knowledge and salvation. Therefore, if a man bathed the Vishweshwara Linga with the waters of this Gyanoda Tirtha, I would destroy his ignorance and impart him with knowledge.'

After fulfilling Ishan's wish, Vishweshwara disappeared. Ishan acquired true knowledge and achieved the blessings of the Supreme Brahman by sipping the sacred water of the wisdom well.[2]

Lingodbhava: The emergence of the Linga of Fire, Jyotirlinga, during the fight for supremacy between Vishnu and Brahma

4

Lingodbhava

The Genesis of the Linga of Fire

Vishwanath Linga being anointed with sandalwood paste

ये शृण्वन्ति मुने! शैवं पुराणं शास्त्रमुत्तमम् ।
ते मनुष्या न मन्तव्या रुद्रा एव न संशयः ॥

'O Sage! Those who listen to Shiva Purana, the noblest of the sacred lore, cease to be mere human beings. They must undoubtedly be considered manifestations of Rudra, a form of Shiva.'

SHIVA PURANA, 'MAHATMYA', CH. 1, VERSE 17

With the arrival of Kaliyuga, the dark age of quarrel and hypocrisy, the inhabitants of earth had abandoned all hopes and strives for the Truth. They began to lead a life of indolence and deceit, often indulging in hedonistic pleasures. This created a problem for the pious Hindu way of life. Therefore, a group of wise sages assembled in Prayagraj, at the sacred confluence of Ganga and Yamuna to discuss the deteriorating social order and to perform *yagna*, a remedial sacrifice.

When the wisest of the sages, Suta, came to know of this great assembly, he too travelled to Prayagraj. He was a disciple of the great sage Vyasa, the arranger of the Vedas and Puranas and the compiler of the epic Mahabharata. Bowing in humility and with joined palms, the sages greeted Suta, saying that since he was an ocean filled with gems of knowledge, he was the right person to dispel their concerns. They humbly asked, 'O Suta, how could the people of Kaliyuga, devoid of all virtues, aspire for salvation? Please tell us the easiest remedy for the immediate destruction of their sins.'[1]

Having heard the anxious sages, Suta told them about worshipping Shiva and his supremacy over all. As the conversation proceeded, the sages then asked that while all the gods were worshipped only in their bodily form, why was Shiva worshipped both in his embodied image and in the form of a phallic emblem, the Linga.

The noble sage narrated the story of Shiva that he had heard from his guru, Sage Vyasa. Suta said that this question was once raised before by Sanatakumara, the brilliant son of Lord Brahma, when he met one of Shiva's attendants Nandikeshwara in the beautiful surroundings of Mount Mandara. Situated in the east of the legendary Mount Meru, Mount Mandara was 11,000 yojana high.[2] It was covered in a variety of trees and herbs and was home to countless animals and singing birds. However, it was so far away from this mortal world that only gods and apsaras could visit it.

A sadhu seeking Shiva in Kashi

According to Nandikeshwara, Shiva was the Supreme Brahman. Therefore, he manifested himself in two forms: in the formless and nameless form of Niskala and in the human form of Sakala. The Niskala nature of Shiva came to be universally worshipped in the form of Linga, the phallic emblem of Shiva. Meanwhile, the Sakala nature of Shiva manifested in the familiar human form: Shiva, dressed in tiger skin, his body smeared with ash, a serpent wrapped around his neck, a crescent moon crowning his forehead and the mighty Ganga springing from his tangled tresses.

A curious Sanatakumara further queried how the practice of worshipping the Shiva Linga began. Nandikeshwara told him that a long time ago, Brahma and Vishnu, the two other gods of the Trinity, had a terrible fight to claim superiority over the other. However, when they reached the point of mutual destruction, the supreme god Shiva, the Parmeshwara, appeared to resolve the dispute.

According to Shiva Purana, the argument began when one day, the great Vedic scholar Brahma went to meet the highest yogi, Vishnu. Resting on Adishesha, the multi-headed serpent, Vishnu was taking a nap, with his consort Lakshmi in attendance. The elderly Brahma flew into a rage because Vishnu had failed to notice his arrival. Castigating Vishnu for his disrespectful conduct, Brahma said, 'Why are you lying here like an arrogant person? Get up, O dear, because I am your Lord. Expiatory rites are ordained for that spiteful wretch who behaves like a big-headed fool at the visit of an honourable elderly person.'[3]

Though fuming within, Vishnu tried to remain calm. He politely asked Brahma to sit next to him and requested him to shed his anger. However, a furious Brahma did not stop there. He continued, 'Dear Vishnu, I am to be honoured greatly. I am the creator of the world. O dear one, the whole universe is situated within me, but your way of thinking is like that of a thief.'[4]

Vishnu lost his patience. The dispute escalated into a full-blown fight. Vishnu was shooting unbearable arrows targeting Brahma while the latter was hurling deadly weapons at Vishnu. Their attendants also joined in. Finally, Vishnu took out the most destructive Maheshwara weapon to kill Brahma, and Brahma hurled at Vishnu his Pashupata weapon, which had thousands of spikes that blazed like ten thousand suns.

The frightful devas stood and watched the turn of events from heaven. They realized they must do something to save the universe from annihilation. So, in their flying chariots, they swiftly rushed to Mount Kailasa, the abode of Shiva. They knew only Shiva, the master of all creation and annihilation, could stop this destructive war.

Priests offering a garland made of Rudraksha beads to the Holy Lord

When the frightened devas arrived at Kailasa, they saw the trident-bearing Shiva sitting in his familiar pose with his right leg resting on his left knee. He was surrounded by noble sages who extolled him with Vedic hymns while his Ganas gently fanned with a flabellum. Sitting with his consort Uma, another name of Parvati, the Parameshwara raised his palm to bless his panicked visitors.

As Parvati, with her sweet smile and honey-like speech, tried to console the terrified devas, Shiva said that he was aware of the terrible fight between Brahma and Vishnu and that he was ready to go to the battlefield.

He immediately assembled his commanders and attendants. The Supreme Lord, accompanied by Parvati and his two sons, Ganesha and Kartikeya, led the march. They were followed by a legion of commanders and attendants, bedecked in their ornaments and arms. Shiva's warriors trooped ahead, displaying colourful banners and uproariously playing the drums and other musical instruments. Indra and other devas followed Shiva's marching legion.

However, at first sight of the battlefield, Shiva miraculously disappeared into the sky. His perplexed followers did not know what to do next. So they looked into the sky where Vishnu's Maheshwara weapon and Brahma's Pashupata weapon were raining fire capable of burning the three worlds. What happened next was absolutely astounding.

First, they watched Shiva dissolve into his bodiless form, transforming into a gigantic column of fire. Then, the fiery weapons of Brahma and Vishnu soon fell into this blazing linga of fire. With their powerful weapons seized, the two warring gods were compelled to stop fighting. They confusingly looked up and down and then agreed to find the beginning and the end of the column of fire. Vishnu assumed the form of a boar to dig down to the roots of the column, while Brahma transformed himself into a swan, flying up to the top of the column. Vishnu soon realized that burrowing up to the roots of the fiery column that reached the netherworlds was impossible. Having exhausted himself, he conceded defeat and returned to the battlefield.

Meanwhile, Brahma, as a swan, continued his endless flight to the top. During his flight, he saw Shiva's favourite Ketaki flower mysteriously falling from above. So, he asked the flower where it was falling from. The Ketaki flower replied that it had been falling for a long time.

The swan-formed Brahma now realized that reaching the top of this fiery column was impossible. So he said to the flower,

Some parents bring their daughter's wedding sarees to be blessed by Lord Vishwanath.

'Dear friend, you must do as I desire. It would help if you told Vishnu that you had witnessed Brahma reaching the top of the column.'[5]

Brahma returned to the battlefield with the Ketaki flower, reassuring himself that a small falsehood was permissible under challenging times. Furthermore, he wanted to enjoy the sight of a dejected Vishnu, confessing to Shiva his inability to reach the roots of the fire column. Brahma victoriously informed Shiva that he had reached the top. The Ketaki flower also testified to Brahma's falsehood.

However, Parmeshwara, now in his embodied form, knew of Brahma's deception. It was Vishnu who spoke first. Prostrating before Shiva, he confessed that his arrogance and delusion prompted him to embark on a futile journey to the bottom of the Linga of Light.

The compassionate Lord was pleased. He blessed Vishnu, saying he would have a status equal to him because he had adhered to the Truth. Therefore, the people would make his idols and temples to worship him and organize festivals to sing his glory.

Then Mahadeva turned towards the deceitful Brahma. With a ferocious gaze from the middle of his eyebrows, he produced a powerful figure called Bhairava and ordered him to sever the fifth head of Brahma. It was from this head that Brahma had uttered the lie. Bhairava followed the orders. At that point, Vishnu intervened and stopped Bhairava from inflicting further injury on Brahma. He pleaded with Shiva to show compassion and not humiliate Brahma further.

Shiva said that leaving an offender unpunished would set a wrong precedent. Brahma wanted to become a superior God through falsehood. Therefore, Shiva ruled that people would not worship him, and there would be no temples or festivals commemorating him. Shiva then admonished the Ketaki flower for its unethical behaviour by declaring that it would not be included in his worship.

After profound apologies from Brahma and the Ketaki flower, the compassionate Lord relented. After dispensing punishment, the ever-forgiving Shiva also granted a boon to Brahma that he would be the presiding deity in all public and private sacrifices. Then, turning to the Ketaki flower, Shiva said that even if it had been excluded from his worship, it could be used to decorate the canopy over his idol, and his Ganas could wear it.[6]

The King of Serpents, Vasuki, covering the Vishwanath Linga

All the while, devas in heaven were watching Brahma and Vishnu reverentially, standing with folded palms in the heavenly court of Parmeshwara. They performed ritual worship, propitiating Vishweshwara with necklaces, anklets, bracelets, coronets, earrings, sacrificial threads, silk cloth, rings, garlands, flowers, betel leaves, camphor, sandal paste, incense, lamps, white umbrella, fans, banners and other divine offerings.

Shiva, the eternal yogi, had little use for these luxuries. So, he set an example by handing over these precious objects to his attendants. Shiva blissfully said: 'Dear children, I am delighted with your worship on this holy day. Henceforth, this day will be known as Shivaratri... My devotees shall observe fast on Shivaratri during the day and night... They shall worship me with flowers to the extent of their strength. By worshipping me on the day of Shivaratri, the devotees shall have the same benefit as year-long worship. This is when the virtue of devotion to me increases like the tide in the ocean on the rise of the moon.'[7]

Finally, Shiva said to Brahma and Vishnu that the column of fire without a top or bottom would henceforth be reduced in size for the sake of worship. Worshipping it in this supreme phallic form would endow a devotee with five types of salvation. First, by worshipping this form of Shiva, a devotee would attain *salokya*, letting him reside on the same planet as the Supreme Lord. Secondly, the devotee would also gain *samipya*, being able to live near the Sacred Lord. The third stage of the liberation would be *sarupya*, assuming the likeness to the divine form of Shiva. The devotee would achieve *sarishti* in the fourth stage, attaining as much splendour as the Supreme Lord. In the final stage of liberation, a Shiva devotee would gain *sayujya*, the union with the Supreme Brahman. These four stages of consciousness would eventually lead a devotee of Shiva to *kaivalya*, the ultimate dissolution of the Self in the Supreme Brahman.

Shiva's vehicle, the Nandi bull, covered in an embroidered stole during Rangbhari Ekadashi

Many devotees whisper their wish in Nandi's ears, hoping it will come true.

A view of the decorated Vishwanath Temple during Rangbhari Ekadashi

Shiva helps Bhagiratha by arresting the mighty flow of Ganga before it arrives on earth

5
The Sacred Waters
Bhagiratha and the Arrival of Ganga

A boat called Jalapari, the water fairy, in the Ganga

यथाऽश्वमेधो यज्ञानां नगानां हिमवान्यथा ।
व्रतानां च यथा सत्यं दानानामभयं यथा ।।
प्राणायामश्च तपसां मंत्राणां प्रणवो यथा ।
धर्माणामप्यहिंसा च काम्यानां श्रीर्यथा वरा ।।
यथाऽत्मविद्या विद्यानां स्त्रीणां गौरी यथोत्तमा ।
सर्वदेवगणानां च यथा त्वं पुरुषोत्तमः ।।
सर्वेषामेव पात्राणां शिवभक्तो यथा वरः ।
तथा सर्वेषु तीर्थेषु गङ्गातीर्थं विशिष्यते ।।

'"Just as a horse sacrifice is the best among all Yagnas, just as Himalaya is the greatest among mountains,
just as truthfulness is the greatest among holy vows,
just as offering freedom from fear is the best among gifts…
just as abstention from violence is the best among all pious activities…
just as Gauri is the most excellent among all women…
just as a devotee of Shiva is the most virtuous among the human beings,
so also Gaṅga is the most excellent among all the Tirthas,"
said Shiva, the Supreme Being to Vishnu.'

SKANDA PURANA, 'KASHI KHANDA', CH. 27, VERSE 70–73

The story of Varanasi cannot be imagined without the free-flowing sacred waters of Ganga. This holy river has not only shaped the spatial characteristics of the city but has also formed the core of Varanasi's spiritual and cultural narrative. The gods performed *leela* (divine acts) on the banks of the holy river. In its tranquil surroundings, the sages held endless deliberations about the nature of the Brahman, and the ancient scholars scripted dharma shastras, epics and treatises on subjects, like astronomy and ayurveda. Undoubtedly, the sacred Ganga has left an enduring imprint on the wisdom of India.

A boat ride in the Ganga

From its origins in Gangotri in the Himalayas to its convergence at Gangasagar in the Bay of Bengal, the Ganga, in its 2,500-km-long course, has some of the most popular pilgrimage centres, attracting Hindus from all parts of the subcontinent. No spiritual quest is fulfilled without a dip in the holy water. Furthermore, those in the twilight of their life come to Ganga to take their last breath, hoping to attain moksha.

Not only does the mighty river provide spiritual solace to faithful Hindus, but it also sustains one of the most fertile and populous regions of India, providing livelihood to millions of priests, pundits, merchants, beggars, boatmen and sellers of fruits, flowers and funeral wood.

On the festival of Ganga Dussehra, at the height of the Indian summer, millions of Indians flock to the shores of the Ganga to take a bath in its sacred waters. The popular belief is that this is the occasion when one can wash off sins accumulated in this and the past lives by bathing in the holy river. However, as things stand today, even Ganga seems stressed by the mindless environmental degradation on its shores.

The story of Ganga's arrival on earth has all the elements of dharmic imagination, divine compassion, familial duty and social piety. The story of its descent has been narrated in various puranas, epics and literary texts. However, no one has narrated it better than Sage Valmiki in his epic, the Ramayana.

The story began when Rama and Lakshmana, the young princes of Ayodhya, were living under the tutelage of the eminent Sage Vishwamitra. While resting on the banks of the Ganga, Rama curiously asked about the origins of the holy river.[1]

Vishwamitra narrated the story to the princes. Their ancestor, the mighty King Sagara of Ayodhya, had two wives and no children. So, along with his wives, Keshini and Sumati, he went to Mount Bhrigu in the Himalayas, the home of the virtuous Sage Bhrigu. He practised gruelling ascesis for a hundred years, which pleased the sage. Bhrigu blessed Keshini with one son, but Sumati gave birth to a long, round cucumber-like egg that produced 60,000 sons.

Years rolled by, and King Sagara's empire grew in all directions. He decided to perform the Ashwamedha Yagna. He sent a sacrificial horse, followed by his brave soldiers, to far-off lands, marking new territories for Sagara's expanding empire. This worried Indra, the king of devas. He felt threatened. So, he stole the horse and hid it near the hermitage of Sage Kapila.

The golden hues of the Ganga

Meanwhile, King Sagara's 60,000 sons searched for the missing horse in all directions. They even dug the earth, causing significant distress to all humans and aquatic beings. Finally, they found the horse near the ashram of Sage Kapila, who was endowed with the powers equivalent to God Vishnu. Sagara's sons angrily dashed towards the great-souled sage, wielding swords, crowbars, ploughs and various trees and boulders. Kapila, who was meditating at that time, flew into a terrible rage. He looked at them with a fiery gaze. Within moments, the 60,000 sons of Sagara were burnt down and turned into a heap of ashes.

After a long wait, Sagara instructed his grandson, Prince Anshumana, to search for his missing sons. Anshumana found the place where his cursed uncles had been burnt to ashes. While grieving for his departed relatives, he looked around for a source of water, so that he could perform their last rites. But he could not find water around. As he searched for a water source, he met Garuda, the king of birds. Garuda told Anshumana that his uncles had been reduced to ashes due to the curse of the powerful Sage Kapila.

Their insolent behaviour was responsible for their misfortune. He suggested that only the heavenly Mother Ganga could bring about their salvation. Ganga, the mighty daughter of Himavan, the king of Himalayas, would have to travel from heaven to earth to wash away their ashes. Despite thousands of years of unfaltering propitiation, Sagara and Anshumana failed to bring down the Ganga. Anshumana's righteous son, King Dilip, could also not accomplish the task.

However, Dilip's son, King Bhagiratha, was determined not to accept defeat. He handed over his kingdom to his ministers and proceeded to the Himalayas to practise the most challenging of ascesis for a thousand years. He stood on one leg, with his hands raised and his senses controlled, having only meagre sustenance, enwrapped in *Panchagani*, the five fires—four in four directions and the sun fire overhead.

Finally, Ganga, the daughter of the king of Himalayas, was pleased with Bhagiratha, assuring him that she was ready to descend on earth. However, there was a problem—no one other than Shiva could sustain the force of her unendurable stream.

Bhagiratha's task was not over yet. He went to Mount Kailasa, where he prayed to Shiva for another thousand years. Finally, Shiva agreed to help him. When Ganga swooped down from heaven, Shiva locked her in the tangled coils of his braids. He released her only when earth could endure its speed and force. The water of Ganga was also sacred because it was falling down the divine head of Shankara.

The idol of Ganga at Dashashwamedha Ghat

It was an extraordinary moment. The gods, devas, sages, gandharvas, apsaras, yakshas and siddhas assembled in the sky in great numbers to witness the descent of the holy Ganga. The tumultuous stream of Ganga's crystal waters with a whitish froth and silver clouds now followed the chariot-riding Bhagiratha. Valmiki, the author of Ramayana, has lyrically described this extraordinary journey to the site of Bhagiratha's dead ancestors.

A devotee lighting lamps on the ghats of Ganga, to seek blessings

'The waters of the holy Ganga sometimes rose high in the air, sometimes flowed tortuously, sometimes broadened out, sometimes dashed against the rocks and sometimes spouted upwards afterwards falling to the ground; that pure water capable of removing sin looked delightful flowing on the surface of the earth. Then the celestial sages and heavenly musicians and the denizens of the earth, reverently touched that sacred stream falling from the locks of Shiva.'[2]

Finally, Bhagiratha's chariot, followed by Ganga, reached the sea and entered the lower regions of Patala, where he mournfully gazed at the heaps of ashes of his 60,000 ancestors. The sacred stream of Ganga flooded the ashes, washing off their sins and leading them to moksha. As Bhagiratha performed the funeral rites of the sons of Sagara, Brahma, the father of humankind, appeared on the scene. He admired the colossal accomplishment of Bhagiratha, saying: 'O King, as long as the waters of the sea continue on this Earth, so long shall the sons of King Sagara live in heaven. Henceforth, O Great Sovereign, Ganga shall be your eldest daughter and be known by your name throughout the Earth. This sacred river shall be named Ganga, Tripathaga and Bhagirathai.'[3]

An invocation to Mother Ganga

A young priest immersed in performing Varanasi's famous Ganga aarti at Dashashwamedha Ghat

Ganga aarti at Dashashwamedha Ghat is a sight to behold

The dance of Shiva and Parvati at Manikarnika

6

The End of the Road

Moksha at Manikarnika

The temple of Ratneshwar Mahadev, popularly known as Kashi Karvat Temple

अनेकजन्मजनितं कर्मसूत्रनियंत्रणम्
उन्मुच्य यत्र मुक्ताः स्युः सैषा श्रीमणिकर्णिका ॥

'This is the glorious Manikarnika, where devotees become liberated after disengaging themselves from the bondage of Karma arising in the course of many births.'

SKANDA PURANA, 'KASHI KHANDA', CH. 33, VERSE 112

As recounted previously, the city of Kashi is blessed by Shiva and Parvati. The popular belief is that the divine couple would ensure the material and spiritual well-being of those who came to reside in Kashi. This lore of Shiva and Parvati has shaped the physical, intellectual and spiritual landscape of Kashi. In Hinduism, a mortal being is expected to perform their prescribed duties and then seek salvation.

In the Hindu tradition, attaining moksha is the ultimate goal of human existence. It is liberation from the worldly existence, the *samsara*. An *atman* (individual soul), suffering from ignorance and illusion, has to go through an endless cycle of birth, death and rebirth. The moksha is the permanent release from this cycle of suffering caused by the physical world. It is a state of spiritual unity with the ultimate reality, the Supreme Brahman.

According to the Hindu tradition, a virtuous individual living in one of India's seven sacred cities (Ayodhya, Mathura, Haridwar, Kashi, Kanchi, Ujjain and Dwarka) could attain freedom from the cycle of rebirth. Even among these seven cities, Kashi is considered the holiest of all. Dying in Kashi is considered auspicious because as per Shiva's vow, he would

Manikarnika Ghat, the gateway to moksha

ensure that anyone who came to live and die in Kashi would be released from the agonizing cycle of life and death.

According to Kashi Khanda, at the time of death, Shiva chants the 'Taraka Brahman Mantra' in the right ear of all creatures, thus liberating them. Consequently, the departing soul finally submerges into the eternal Brahman.[1]

Manikarnika is the *mahashmashan*, the great cremation ground of Kashi. It is one of Kashi's most sacred spaces. For millennia, the funeral pyres have burned here non-stop, round the clock. However, if there is a rare break and there are no dead bodies for cremation, flames are kept alive by the ceremonial burning of the Kusha grass.

As the legend has it, after Shiva and Parvati happily settled down in Anandakanana, they had a desire to create another being. One day, while sitting with Parvati, Shiva glanced at his left limb. From there emerged a person with the most handsome features. His calm appearance personified *sattva* (righteousness). His majestic reach transcended the mighty oceans. He had the brilliance of a blue diamond. His eyes resembled a lotus flower and his skin sparkled like gold. He also had long and mighty arms. He was the most handsome being in the three worlds, exuding the sweet fragrance of his divine body around him. He possessed all the good qualities and practised all kinds of arts. Hence, he was to be known as Purushottama, the best among men.

Looking appreciatively, Shiva said to his creation, 'O Mahavishnu, you would be exhaling the knowledge of Vedas. That knowledge would guide your actions.' As Shiva and Shakti left the scene, Lord Vishnu bowed his head and mulled over his future course of action. Finally, he decided to dig a pond. It was hard work, leading him to sweat profusely. The lotus pond he dug with his discus was soon filled with his sweat. It was called *Chakrapushkarni*.[2]

And there, Lord Vishnu sat motionless, performing his penance for 55,000 years. Pleased with his resolute tapas, Shiva and Parvati arrived there and said, 'This is the greatness of penance. What a wonderful way to stabilize the mind and achieve patience. O Mahavishnu, that is enough. Now ask for your boon.'

The four-armed Lord opened his lotus eyes and said, 'O Deva of Devas, O chief among the divine beings, I wish to see you here in Anandakanana, always in the company of Bhavani.'

The mahashamshana, or the great cremation ground, of Manikarnika

Shiva was extremely delighted. He replied, 'O Janardana, let everything turn out as you have wished.'

Manikarnika Ghat

In a mood of unparallel ecstasy, Shiva shook his serpent-adorned head so vigorously that his gem-studded earring Manikarnika fell at that spot. Shiva then told Vishnu that this sacred expanse of water would henceforth be known as the salvation-granting Manikarnika.

Looking at Shiva's beneficence, Vishnu further asked, 'O mighty Shiva, beloved of the Daughter of the Mountain King, let this spot be the greatest of all salvation-granting spots. And since you have dropped your brilliantly shining gemstone earring, let this place be famous by another name, the luminous city of Kashi. So let all the living creatures, beginning from Brahma and ending with a blade of grass, attain salvation here in Kashi.'

'Let it be so, O Madhusudana,' said Shiva.[3]

Morning at the cremation ghat of Manikarnika

Kashi: Illuminated with the light of self-knowledge

Part 2

RITUALS, RENOVATIONS AND REFLECTIONS

Prime Minister Narendra Modi inaugurating the new temple complex in 2021

7

Reviving the Splendour

The Making of Kashi Vishwanath Dham

One of the ancient temples found near the Vishwanath Temple after the demolition of unauthorized properties in November 2018

'I visited the Vishwanath Temple last evening, and when I walked through those lanes, these thoughts touched me. If a stranger dropped from above onto this great temple, he had to consider what we, as Hindus, were, would he not be justified in condemning us? Is not this great temple a reflection of our character? I speak feelingly, as a Hindu. Is it right that the lanes of our sacred temple should be as dirty as they are? The houses round about are built anyhow. The lanes are tortuous and narrow. If even our temples are not models of roominess and cleanliness, what can our self-government be?'

MAHATMA GANDHI AT THE INAUGURAL FUNCTION OF
THE BANARAS HINDU UNIVERSITY (BHU), 4 FEBRUARY 1916[1]

Almost a hundred years after Mahatma Gandhi gave this speech at the inaugural function of BHU, when I visited the Kashi Vishwanath Temple in February 2017, things had hardly changed. The lanes were narrow and tortuous. There were no signs of roominess or cleanliness. Perhaps, they were more congested due to unrestrained encroachment and filthier due to the presence of cows and huge crowds. The famous Vishwanath lane was full of the previous evening's litter, with paper and plastic bags strewn everywhere. In the haze of the early dawn, I had to step carefully to escape the piles of cow dung.

Multi-storey houses dwarfed the main temple. One of the house owners had put up an iron beam right on the temple's boundary wall. The temple sat in a narrow courtyard with hardly any space to move around. There were no facilities for the pilgrims. On busy festival days, the devotees had to wait in queues for up to five hours without drinking water or having access to toilet amenities.

Moreover, the temple structure was in a bad shape. It was covered in glossy chemical paint, harming its stone structure. The golden spire had virtually gone black. The temple doors, as well as the ceiling, were covered in black soot. Even the current temple structure that Queen Ahilya Bai built in 1777 was perforated to lay water pipes and electricity cables in many places.

The situation in the surrounding lanes was even worse. Local businesses had occupied old temples. One of the temples had been converted into a tea and samosa shop. A homoeopathic doctor had built a multi-storey clinic in another temple premise. A sewer pipe could be seen running through the foundation of an intricately carved ancient temple. What shocked me the most was a goat wandering inside a derelict temple and a cat resting over a Shiva Linga.

Another ancient temple hidden inside an unauthorized house

For over 200 years, India's sacred Kashi Vishwanath Temple had survived on a 3,000 sq. ft piece of land, equivalent to a four-bedroom flat. The temple compound was tightly surrounded by an old delapidated wall. A visit to one of the most revered sites of Hinduism was undoubtedly an unpleasant experience. So in 2014, when PM Narendra Modi arrived in Varanasi to represent it in the Indian parliament, he must have noticed the pathetic state of affairs. He vowed to change it.

He proposed a ₹339-crore project called the Kashi Vishwanath Dham to remove encroachments, renovate the temple, redesign the temple complex and finally create a wide corridor from the Ganga to the temple. As a result, the government acquired more than 400 properties, and the displaced residents were offered generous compensation, and in some cases it was up to three times above the prevailing market rates.

When I visited Varanasi in November 2018, the demolition work was being carried out manually. There were mountains of rubble that could only be cleared by using donkeys because removal trucks could not enter those narrow streets. It looked like an impossible task.

The biggest surprise of the project was finding more than 78 ancient temples subjected to illegal encroachment. Many of these temples had been hidden behind private properties for so long that residents had entirely forgotten about them. One of the most prominent temples was a virtual replica of the present Vishwanath Temple.

Today, as people walk along the 50-m-wide corridor from the Ganga and approach the temple courtyard, they notice a black stone statue of the Holkar Queen Ahilya Bai, who reconstructed the present Vishwanath Temple between 1777–80.

PM Modi was following a long tradition of rebuilding and renovating the Kashi Vishwanath Temple. The temple had a chequered history of demolition and resurrection. Iconoclastic Islamic invaders damaged or demolished the temple at least six times between the twelfth and seventeenth centuries. But the people and the priests of Varanasi did not rest until the temple was resurrected again. In 1194, Qutub-ud-din Aibak, the chief commander of Muhammad Ghori, invaded Varanasi. The raid was particularly brutal. Aibak carried off the looted treasures on 1,400 camels and 'converted about thousand idol-temples into houses for the Musalmans'.[2] Later on, Queen Razia (1236–40) built a mosque over the demolished Vishweshwar Temple. The temple was also destroyed by the Sharqi rulers of the nearby Jaunpur, Feroz Shah Tughlaq and Sikandar Lodhi.

Alamgir mosque at Panchaganga Ghat was built by the Mughal king Aurangzeb after the demolition of Bindu Madhav Temple.

We have ample hints that for many years, even during the reign of Akbar, Varanasi seemed to have no proper structure dedicated to Vishweshwara. We find a prominent public figure of Kashi, the Hindu scholar Narayan Bhatt, agonizing over the absence of Vishweshwara temple in Varanasi. He even advised Hindus to continue worshipping Shiva on the site of the demolished temple. In his famous book *Tristhalisetu,* he wrote:

> Even if the Linga of Vishweshwara is taken off somewhere and another is brought in and established by human hands, on account of the difficulty of the times, whatever is established in that place should be worshipped... And if, owing to the power of foreign rulers, there is no Linga at all in that place, even so, the Dharma of the place should be observed... Even if the absence of the foremost Linga of light, Vishweshwara, worship should be offered to another Linga put in its place.[3]

This not only suggests the non-existence of the temple of Vishweshwara, at least in part of Narayana Bhatt's lifetime (1514–95), but also tells us that the Linga of Vishweshwara was removed by foreign rulers. Later, Bhatt met the influential finance minister of Akbar, Todarmal, who was a devout Hindu and owned a large haveli adjacent to the Vishwanath Temple. Finally, in 1585, Akbar allowed Bhatt and Todarmal to reconstruct a grand temple in Varanasi. Also, Raja Man Singh, another of Akbar's influential courtiers, is said to have financed the construction of a temple. The remnants of this temple can still be seen on the western wall of the Gyan Vapi Mosque.[4]

Todarmal's grand temple only survived for 84 years before it was demolished by Akbar's great-grandson, Aurangzeb, in September 1669. Those were the darkest times for the residents of the city. He had reimposed *jizya,* an Islamic tax on non-Muslims; introduced a pilgrimage tax for visitors; and also renamed Varanasi as Muhammadabad.[5]

The attempts to reclaim the site and reconstruct the Vishwanath Temple began a few decades after Aurangzeb's death in 1707. Taking advantage of the fast-eroding Mughal authority, Malhar Rao Holkar, the Maratha ruler of Indore, planned to demolish the Gyan Vapi Mosque to build a new temple in 1742. But he could not proceed due to the stiff opposition from Nawab Safdar Jung of Awadh, who had become a mighty figure in the disintegrating Mughal empire. The proposal to demolish the mosque terrified the 'Dravid' Brahmins of Kashi so much that they petitioned the Maratha ruler not to embark upon this course.[6]

Meanwhile, the descendants of Akbar's trusted lieutenants, including Raja Man Singh, the Kachawaha ruler of Jaipur, were also

The sixteenth-century Man Mandir Ghat, built by Raja Man Singh, a trusted courtier of the Mughal king Akbar

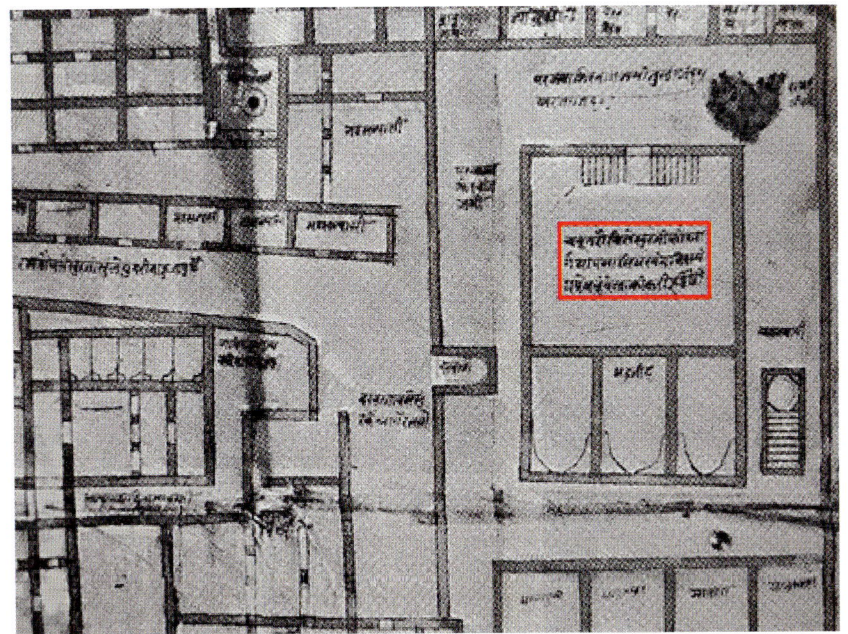

(From left to right) An eighteenth-century map of Kashi in Jaipur's Kachawaha royal family archives, along with present-day Google Earth map of the same location. The current *wazukhana* (the ablution pond) is located at the same position where Vishweshwara platform can be seen marked in the Jaipur map (on the left).

planning to rebuild and restore the glory of prominent religious places that had suffered during Aurangzeb's reign. Maharaja Bishan Singh and Sawai Jai Singh II appointed surveyors to map religious cities, like Banaras (now Varanasi), Allahabad (now Prayagraj), Vrindavan and Ujjain. Interestingly, the survey map of Kashi is quite revealing. This map, titled '*Taraha Kasi ji ki*' or the 'Plan of Kashi', number 191, was published in the catalogue of the official archives of the Jaipur ruling family.[7] It provides critical evidence about the state of Gyan Vapi Mosque and the Hindu religious sites around it. It also shows a 21-foot-wide circumambulation path around the mosque. We know that circumambulation of a sacred place is an established Hindu religious practice. On this map, one can see the three domes of Aurangzeb's mosque. However, the most crucial information is recorded in the courtyard of the mosque. It is described as '*Bissesur ji ko chabutaro*' or 'the raised platform of Vishweshwara'.

This platform is marked right in front of the three domes of the Gyan Vapi Mosque. But the wazukhana stands in its place now.[8] The historical significance of the Jaipur map lies in the fact that there is no existence of the Vishwanath Temple next to the mosque. Historian Madhuri Desai said, 'This meant that the enclosure of the Gyan Vapi Mosque retained its attraction as a sacred site and pilgrimage destination. The platform of the mosque was worshipped, and the act further sustained the memory of the temple.'[9] She cites the example of a Bengali businessman Bijayram Sen, who took a family of pilgrims to worship Vishweshwara and the surrounding deities in the year 1768. This means that in the decades following the death of Aurangzeb, some sort of Hindu religious activities were continuing in and around the Gyan Vapi Mosque.

Following the Battle of Buxar in 1764, the political situation changed dramatically. The Mughal Emperor Shah Alam was forced to cede Banaras to the East India Company. However, the rulers of Banaras, Raja Balwant Singh and Raja Chait Singh, resisted the East India Company's dominance. At one point, Chait Singh arrested Governor Warren Hastings, but then he committed the historical mistake that many Indian kings had committed in the past—he let the captured enemy go. The Company forces soon returned to punish and dethrone Chait Singh.

In those years of turmoil, when no one had complete control over Banaras, Rani Ahilya Bai fulfilled her life ambition by resurrecting the Vishwanath Temple in 1777.[10] However, unlike her father-in-law, Mahlar Rao Holkar, demolishing the Gyan Vapi Mosque was not on her agenda. Instead, she only managed to build a small temple on the adjacent piece of land, covering an area of just 3,000 sq. ft.

While photographing inside the present-day Vishwanath Temple, I found two intriguing figures carved inside the sanctum sanctorum. One of them was a figure of a lady with large bell-shaped earrings, a triple-layered necklace and a tiara on her head. She sat with closed eyes and folded hands, praying to Lord Vishwanath.

The newly built Kashi Vishwanath Corridor has a statue of Queen Ahilya Bai Holkar of Indore, who built the Vishwanath Temple in 1777.

On the other side of the door, I found a meditating figure of an elderly gentleman, with a thick moustache. He was wrapped in a shawl with a

Carved inside the sanctum sanctorum of the present-day Vishwanath Temple are two intriguing figures facing the sacred Shiva Linga. The figure on the right is perhaps of Queen Ahilya Bai herself, and that of the man on her left could be that of her mentor and father-in-law, Malhar Rao Holkar.

The gateway to the Kashi Vishwanath Corridor

decorative necklace of broad beads. His elegant posture suggested he must have been a nobleman.

I enquired the temple priests about the figures. They said one of the figures was that of Goddess Parvati. However, Parvati could already be seen in a carved image where she was riding on Nandi with Shiva. Moreover, if the figure was that of Parvati, then who was the elderly gentleman sitting on the other side of the door? He was certainly not Shiva. The baffled priests had no answer. I spoke to several religious and spiritual figures and some visitors, but nobody could give a satisfactory answer.

My closest guess was that the female figure was that of Queen Ahilya Bai. The elderly man might have been her mentor and father-in-law, Malhar Rao Holkar. We have one contemporary portrait of Malhar Rao, painted in 1770. The portrait featured a thick moustache and a large build similar to the figure carved on the marble wall of the Kashi Vishwanath Temple. We also know that Malhar Rao, who died in 1766, had also attempted to rebuild the temple. I discussed this puzzling aspect with one of the leading chroniclers of Varanasi, Professor Rana P.B. Singh of BHU. He endorsed my view.[11]

It is probable that the Queen must have been quite keen to have an evidence of her involvement in reconstructing one of the most prominent landmarks of the Hindu civilization. Remember, those were uncertain times—the Mughals were retreating and the British were aggressively trying to occupy India. So, it is remarkable that a Maratha queen came from at least 1,000 km away to restore the lost glory of a significant landmark.

All the attempts to restore the temple across centuries finally came to fruition when PM Modi presented the renovated temple to the nation on 13 December 2021 in a nationally televised grand ceremony. He walked through the corridor with a goblet of Gangajal in his hands to offer it to Baba Vishwanath. Next, he performed Rudrabhisheka, presided over by the temple priest, Pandit Shrikant Mishra. It was an extraordinary moment in the 75-year-long history of the Republic of India—an Indian PM inaugurating a renovated Hindu temple. No Indian PM has done it before.

The new temple complex covers an area of 500,000 sq. ft. It has over 20 buildings, including a facilitation hub, a Vedic study centre, a museum and elaborate arrangements for refreshments for the pilgrims. Today, the renovated Vishwanath Temple can easily be considered one of India's finest and cleanest Hindu temples.

Prime Minister Narendra Modi arriving to perform puja inside the Vishwanath Temple during the inauguration ceremony of Kashi Vishwanath Dham project.

Prime Minister Modi performing Rudrabhisheka

Prime Minister Modi offering milk to Baba Vishwanath during Rudrabhisheka

Details of the gold-plated spire of the Vishwanath Temple

Maharaja Ranjit Singh of Punjab donated 1,000 kg gold to the Kashi Vishwanath Temple during his visit in 1835.

Shiva preaches Adi Yoga to the seven celestial sages

8

In Three Aartis

A Day in the Life of Shri Kashi Vishwanath

Priests performing Saptarishi Aarti, with floral decorations on Shiva Linga

ॐ त्र्यम्बकं यजामहे सुगन्धिं पुष्टिवर्धनम् ।
उर्वारुकमिव बन्धनान्मृत्योर्मुक्षीय मामृतात् ।।

'We worship the three-eyed One (Shiva), who is fragrant and who nourishes all.
Like the fruit is liberated from the bondage of the stem, may we be liberated from death, from mortality.'

MAHAMRITYUNJAYA MANTRA, RIG VEDA

SAPTARISHI AARTI

Saptarishi aarti is one of the major rituals performed in the Kashi Vishwanath Temple since ancient times. It is believed that Lord Shiva prescribed this aarti to the seven ancient sages, namely Kratu, Pulaha, Pulastya, Atri, Angiras, Vashishtha and Bhrigu. (Though their names frequently differ in various ancient texts.)

In the Hindu tradition, they are believed to be the sons of Brahma who conquered death with their yogic powers. They are also described as Brahma rishis, the knower of the Brahman, because of their divine knowledge. A story in Mahabharata tells us that even during the *Mahapralaya*, the great deluge, when the entire humanity was destroyed, these seven sages were saved by Lord Vishnu when he appeared in the form of a fish. They had a long life, surviving all four ages starting from Satya Yuga.

The Saptarishis had a long association with Shiva, who once summoned them to dissuade Parvati from marrying him. Shiva thought Parvati would be unable to cope with his unconventional way of living on cremation grounds in the company of awkward friends and attendants.

Following Shiva's instructions, the seven sages went to Himavana in the present-day Himalayas, where Parvati was performing penance to win Shiva's heart. The Saptarishis tried to discourage Parvati by arguing that Shiva, owing to his unconventional ways of living, was unworthy of her. Besides, he had no home and lived with ghosts and goblins.

Parvati firmly rebuffed the Saptarishis, saying even if the sun rose in the West and the mountain Meru moved from its place,

Priests placing silver-plated serpents on the Linga

Priests in a state of trance during the Saptarishi Aarti

her determination to marry Shiva could not be reversed. When the Saptarishis informed Shiva of Parvati's resolve, he relented and married her.

The close association of Shiva and the Saptarishis is further confirmed by another event that took place in Varanasi. The pundits in Varanasi believe that it was here that Shiva blessed the celestial sages with the supreme knowledge of yoga. They could protect and guide the universe to the righteous path with this knowledge and its boundless energy. He then instructed them to go around the world to spread this yogic knowledge.

The idea of leaving Kashi, the abode of Shiva and the most beautiful places on earth, saddened the sages. They lamented and begged Shiva not to ask them to leave Kashi. The most compassionate Lord then allowed them to stay in Kashi and handed them a daily yogic ritual, so that they would be able to summon him to protect the universe. Since then, the story goes that these seven priests and their succeeding generations have been summoning Shiva every evening to the Kashi Vishwanath Temple by performing Saptarishi Aarti.

Witnessing Saptarishi Aarti was an unforgettable experience. Amidst a jostling crowd, I took my position at the western door of the sanctum sanctorum to film and photograph the hour-long process of the Saptarishi Aarti. The aarti began with the offerings of water, milk, yoghurt, honey and the sacred ash to the Holy Lord. The Linga was anointed with sandalwood paste and colourful flowers. A group of priests carefully placed a multi-headed silver-plated serpent upon the linga. Their chants remained mostly indecipherable under the belief that this communication between the celestial sages and the Supreme Lord was beyond the comprehension of ordinary mortals.

Leading the final stage of the Saptarishi Aarti was a priest of an immense figure with large red eyes, a broad forehead and a triple sandalwood mark. His black ponytail was tightly pulled back, and his hairy chest was covered with multiple rudraksha necklets. He was followed by six other priests.

While photographing the climax, my focus was to capture the spiritual ecstasy that filled the sanctum. In the final stage of the aarti, the seven priests shook their heads vigorously and swung their lamps around the deity amidst the amplified sounds of bells and *damaru* (double-sided drums). The head priest almost fell into a trance, invoking the protective energy of Vishweshara, the lord of the world. Sitting outside the gilded doors of the sanctum sanctorum was a crowd of emotional devotees, who were convinced of being blessed by the benevolent Lord.

Meanwhile, the space inside the temple compound virtually withered away, making human movement nearly impossible. It was indeed an unforgettable spectacle of sounds and sights. Amidst a passionate cacophony of bells, damaru and *shankha* (conch shells), the devotees passionately began chanting '*Har, Har Mahadeva*'.

Hindus believe that with Shiva's blessings, the Saptarishis have attained immortality. Therefore, the ancient Hindu astronomers have celebrated their memory by designating the seven stars of the constellation of Ursa Major as Saptarishis.

Adorning Shiva Linga during Mangala Aarti

MANGALA AARTI

A day at Kashi Vishwanath Temple begins early in the morning at around 3.00 a.m., with a glorious ritual, the Mangala Aarti. One has to book their place in advance by paying a fee online. And those with tickets should arrive at the designated gate at the stipulated time. The hour-long ritual begins with a prayer for the welfare of the world. The presiding priest then summons Lord Vishwanath to bless the entire world and to spread happiness, harmony and peace, knowledge and wisdom.

This is followed by *Shodashopachara* pooja, or worship of sixteen elements. The prayer mantras have been taken from Shukla Yajurveda. While chanting these mantras, the priests invite the Lord through meditation. The sacred Linga is worshiped,

The Holy Lord being offered a milk bath

Shiva Linga being bathed with Ganga's water during Mangala Aarti

Pushp shringar of Shiva Linga during Mangala Aarti

The Shiva Linga being adorned with lamps during Mangala Aarti

The final bow to the revered Lord at the end of the Mangala Aarti

holding a feeling that it has taken the anthropomorphic form. The priests wash his feet, offer him a sip of water, and bathe him in cow milk, yoghurt, butter, honey and raw sugar. Next, the holy Linga is again washed with water from the Ganga and offered fragrant sandalwood paste, clothes and sacred thread. Then Baba Vishwanath, as the people of Varanasi lovingly call him, is offered flowers, fruits and his favourite Bilva leaves. The most trance-inducing highlight of the Mangala Aarti is the enthralling sounds of bells and damarus. The sanctum sanctorum gets filled with the golden and greyish hue of smoke rising from the burning of camphor lamps. Sitting on the four doors of the temple, an ecstatic crowd seems to be filled with devotion and joy.

SHAYAN AARTI

A day at Kashi Vishwanath Temple ends with the Shayan Aarti, when the priests prepare arrangements of night's rest for the Lord. A bed is laid out every night in one corner of the sanctum. It is covered with a red silk bedsheet and a gold-embroidered scarlet quilt. *Khadau* (wooden sandals) are kept next to the bed, and a jug of water is placed nearby in case Baba feels thirsty at night. And then, the devotees of Baba Vishwanath assemble to pray and please the Lord.

Devotees singing the glory of Baba Vishwanath during Shayan Aarti

Shayan Aarti is not devised or performed by trained temple priests. There are no complex mantras and no spiritual invocations. There are no set rituals and no prescribed poojas. The prayers are neither written in any ancient texts nor are they composed in Sanskrit by ancient sages and poets.

A priest presiding over the Shayan Aarti

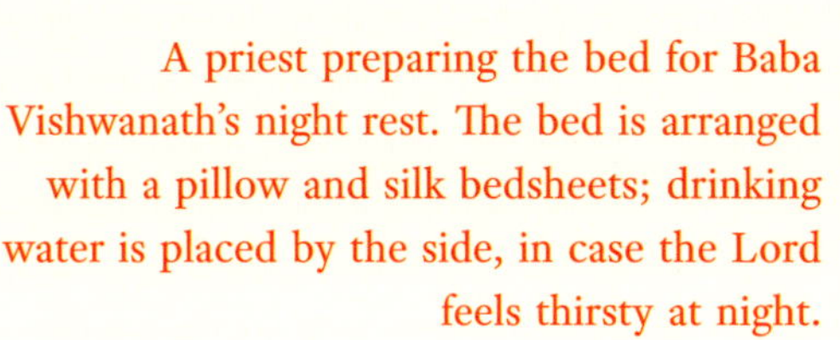

A priest preparing the bed for Baba Vishwanath's night rest. The bed is arranged with a pillow and silk bedsheets; drinking water is placed by the side, in case the Lord feels thirsty at night.

It's people's aarti in people's language, sprinkled with the words of Awadhi, Bhojpuri, Hindi and Sanskrit. It is believed that this aarti was initially sung by the ganas of Shiva, and the people of Kashi have kept this tradition alive. Every night at around 10.00 p.m., the devotees assemble in the court of their beloved Baba Vishwanath and sing his praises. Some locals have been participating in this aarti without a fail for over five decades.

Followers enacting Shiva's wedding procession

It's here that one gets a good glimpse of Kashi's fabled *masti*, the carefree joy. The devotees, singing at the top of their voices, summon their entire energy and boundless dedication to sing the praise of Shiva.

There is also a belief among the people of Kashi that those who participate in the Shayan Aarti will enjoy a sound sleep. People believe that this energetically thrilling prayer helps them forget their anxieties and torments of their everyday life. Having thus abandoned their worries at the door of Baba Vishwanath, the devotees retire to a peaceful night's sleep to begin the next day with renewed vigour and enthusiasm.

Red clouds of sindoor inside the sanctum sanctorum of the temple

9
Shivaratri and Rangbhari Ekadashi
Festivals inside Kashi Vishwanath Temple

Revellers dancing with Shiva's favourite instrument, damaru

न मे दोषरागौ न मे लोभमोहौ
मदो नैव मे नैव मात्सर्यभाव:।
न धर्मो न चार्थो न कामो न मोक्ष:
चिदानन्दरूप: शिवोऽहं शिवोऽहम्।

'Neither do I have hatred, nor attachment, neither greed nor infatuation,
Neither do I have pride, nor feelings of envy and jealousy.
I am not within the bounds of righteousness, wealth, desire and moksha,
I am the ever blissful consciousness; I am Shiva, I am Shiva.'

'NIRVANA SHATKAM', ADI SHANKARACHARYA, VERSE 3

In February 2020, I was privileged to participate in the Shivaratri celebrations inside the Kashi Vishwanath Temple. According to Hindu mythology, Shivaratri is the celebration of the divine union of Shiva and Parvati. The devotees observe fast and perform night-long ritual worship of Shiva. Visiting the Kashi Vishwanath Temple on its busiest day was an unforgettable experience. I was part of a crowd of more than four lakh people, pushing my way towards the sanctum sanctorum. The priest, by now familiar with me, helped me secure a tiny space on the western door of the sanctum sanctorum.

A crowd of priests inside partially blocked my view. On behalf of their privileged *yajmana* (client devotees), they offered all sorts of gifts to the Lord—silk sarees, sweets, fruits, coconuts, vermillion, floral garlands, bael leaves, milk and water. While the privileged ones sat at the doors of the sanctum, a massive crowd kept on jostling for a momentary glimpse of Shri Kashi Vishwanath. Those who were unable to reach the sanctum

Young devotees enjoying Rangbhari Ekadashi

threw from a distance their offerings of milk, water, vermillion, flowers and bael leaves in the direction of the Lord. Half of it fell over those who had occupied the doors. Within minutes, I was totally drenched, and my blue anorak was coloured crimson. Though consistently pushed from behind, here I was, refusing to quit my little corner at the door of the holy sanctum and savouring for more than six hours all the rituals, services and prayers performed on this great night dedicated to Shiva. That night, I witnessed the power of faith—an enormous crowd, almost in a state of ecstasy, seeking the divine intervention of Vishwanath, the lord of the world, to bless their mortal existence.

As the auspicious moment arrived around 3.00 a.m., a priest shouted at me, 'Take away your camera, or it will be ruined. We are going to shower Baba with sindoor.' I was faced with a choice—to save my camera or to capture that rare moment. I chose the latter. As all the priests threw a fistful of sindoor, a cloud of red vermillion filled the entire sanctum. Outside, the crowd broke into hysterical screams of '*Har Har Mahadeva, Har Har Mahadeva!*'

The next time I travelled to Kashi after almost a year-long break, the temple was celebrating its second most important annual festival, Rangbhari Ekadashi. It is believed that after his wedding, Shiva brought his bride, Parvati, to his favourite abode, Kashi, where the newlywed couple received an enormous public welcome. Therefore, every year, a few days before the Hindu festival of Holi, on the eleventh day of the waxing moon in the month of Falgun (March), the people of Kashi celebrate the day as Rangbhari Ekadashi.

On Rangbhari Ekadashi, that year, the entire temple complex was elaborately decorated with flowers. Shiva's bull Nandi was draped in an embroidered stole, and the Gyan Vapi was adorned with red sindoor and colourful flowers. Standing in the middle of the well was a life-size idol of Shiva.

Around sunset, a large number of volunteers assembled at the home of one of the high priests to worship the silver-plated idols of Lord Shiva and Goddess Parvati. Then, a group of volunteers took out a procession, carrying these idols in a decorated palanquin to the Kashi Vishwanath Temple. It looked as if the entire Varanasi was out on the streets. The city was drowned in a sea of joy, with thousands of people singing and dancing, many blowing shankha and playing damarus.

Throughout the procession route, women could be seen assembled on the rooftops. Some held their heads low in reverence and others flung *gulaal*, the dry red powder, over the idols of Shiva and Parvati.

A panoramic view of the renovated temple during Rangbhari Ekadashi

As the procession entered the temple compound, the waiting crowd hysterically roared '*Har Har Mahadev*'. Some of them sprayed gulaal on the palanquin of Shiva and Parvati, leaving a scarlet cloud in the air. Soon, everyone was covered in the fine red powder, and the temple's white marble floor was coloured with red water.

The priests welcomed the idols inside the sanctum sanctorum of the temple. The entire temple complex echoed with the deafening sounds of bells, damarus and the roars of Lord's praise. I could hardly stand on my feet on the slippery, wet floor. Meanwhile, the damaru players had gathered outside the sanctum sanctorum, presenting an exhilarating demonstration of energy, skills and passion for the Moksha-giving Holy Lord and the life-sustaining Mother Goddess.

The newly built outer courtyard of the temple

The majestic view of the temple after renovation

The grand entrance gate of the temple

A portrait of Tulsidas placed in his house at Tulsi Ghat

10
Tulsidas
Assimilating Rama and Shiva

The house at Tulsi Ghat where Tulsidas is believed to have stayed

न जानामि योगं जपं नैव पूजां
नतोऽहं सदा सर्वदा शम्भु तुभ्यम् ।
जराजन्मदुःखौघतातप्यमानम्
प्रभो पाहि आपन्नमामीश शम्भो ।।

'I do not know how to perform yoga, japa or puja.
I always at all times only bow down to You, O Shambhu.
Please protect me from the sorrows of birth, old age, and the sins which lead to suffering.
Please protect me O Lord from afflictions; protect me O My Lord Shambhu.'

RAMACHARITAMANAS, 'UTTARA KHANDA', VERSE 107–8

The story of Varanasi would remain incomplete without mentioning Tulsidas, one of the most illustrious figures of the Hindu Renaissance. His life was an extraordinary story of an unfortunate boy abandoned at birth by his father, a boy who later grew up to become one of the most prominent figures in Kashi, leading the Hindu religious revival. He also brought about a unique social transformation by creating hope in a society oppressed by despotic rulers.

Tulsidas also emphasized reconciliation between the various streams of Hinduism, particularly between the rival followers of Shiva and Vishnu. Though an influential exponent of Vaishnav tradition and an ardent devotee of Rama, Tulsidas had vividly sung the glory of Shiva. It was indeed the assimilating influence of Kashi that must have inspired Tulsidas to integrate the legends of Shiva and Rama joyfully.

An interesting aspect of Tulsidas's epic *Ramcharitamanas* is that, instead of Rama, it begins with the story of Shiva. The saga of Sati's resolve to marry Shiva, and their unusual wedding after the intervention of the gods and the seven celestial sages is recounted in the epic in great detail. Shiva is also one of the four narrators of the *Ramcharitamanas*.

Towards the end of the epic, Tulsidas, in the Lanka Khanda, hints at the Shaiv and Vaishnav rivalry. Before crossing the ocean to invade Sri Lanka, Lord Rama worships Shiva. Sugriva, the leader of Rama's monkey army, invited many sages for this special

Khadau of Tulsidas

The peepul tree at Tulsi Ghat. This is where Tulsidas is said to have composed the last chapters of his great epic *Ramacharitamanas*.

occasion. After the ritual worship of Shiva, Lord Rama declares, 'No one else is dearer to me than Shiva. If any of my devotees remain hostile to Shiva, he would not be able to attain me even in his dreams. Those who worship me and oppose Shiva are half-brained idiots, and they would end up in hell.'[1]

In the Uttar Khanda, the last chapter of *Ramcharitamanas,* Tulsidas composed one of the finest odes to Shiva, the Rudrashtakam: '*Namami Shamishan Nirvana Roopam* (O Lord, who is present as Ishnaa, I prostrate before you, who is the embodiment of Nirvana, the salvation through the union of Atman with Brahman).' It is a beautiful Sanskrit hymn of eight stanzas portraying Shiva's divine qualities and deeds.[2]

The *Ramacharitamanas* soon became one of the most influential texts of Hinduism, particularly in North India. Tulsidas had begun composing it in the spring of 1575 in Ayodhya. Having finished the first three chapters in Ayodhya, he had moved to Varanasi. In the fourth chapter, the Kishkindha Khanda, he talks about the demon king Ravana kidnapping Sita. A distraught Rama, with his brother Lakshmana, is meanwhile searching for his missing wife. Here, Tulsidas breaks the story and suddenly, totally out of context, begins to sing the praise of Kashi: 'Why not savour Kashi, the abode of Shambhu and Bhavani, the place of final liberation, the mine of spiritual knowledge and the destroyer of sins.'

Tulsidas's arrival in Kashi was also not free from trouble. His decision to compose the *Ramcharitamanas* in Awadhi infuriated many Sanskrit scholars of Kashi. They wondered how someone could dare to retell sage Valmiki's great Sanskrit epic, Ramayana, in a vernacular dialect. Perhaps due to this harassment, Tulsidas had to stay at three different places in Kashi. He finally moved to the city's outskirts at the southernmost Assi Ghat, where he composed the last four chapters of the *Ramcharitamanas*.

The area where Tulsidas stayed is now called Tulsi Ghat. One has to climb a set of steep stairs from the Ganga to reach the place. There stands a huge peepul tree, with three adjacent shrines of Shiva. The tree looks ancient, and one can imagine Tulsidas sitting underneath and composing the verses of his divine poem.

The narrow staircase leads to the two-storey quarter, which was Tulsidas's living space. The floor has a small personal shrine that Tulsidas had set up. His bed is set in a locked enclosure. Placed on this bed is a painting of the poet-saint, which was said to have been painted by one of his disciples after his death. I met Pandit Vishwambhar Nath Mishra, the thirteenth Mahant of Tulsi Ghat and Sankat Mochan Hanuman Temple. Interestingly, he is not a saffron-clad sadhu but a professor of

Tulsi Akhara, a wrestling training centre, is believed to have been set up by Tulsidas.

electronics engineering at BHU. He allowed us to photograph the khadau of Tulsidas and the blade of the oars of his boat. He informed us that most of the Tulsi Ghat idols had been placed by Tulsidas himself.[3]

We do not know how *Ramcharitamanas* was circulated among its readers. However, we know that Tulsidas began to narrate the story of Rama in public gatherings. The residents of Kashi flocked to these assemblies in large numbers. Tulsidas soon became a prominent figure in Kashi's luminous world of learning. He also established the famous Sankat Mochan Hanuman Temple on the sacred spot, where he is said to have had a personal encounter with Lord Hanuman. Legend has it that Lord Hanuman used to attend Tulsidasa's Ramkatha assemblies, all the while hidden in the guise of an old man.

He also pioneered the tradition of Ramlila, the dramatic public presentation of the story of Rama. In the sixteenth century Banaras, the public enactment of Ramlila must have been a great source of entertainment and a rallying strategy to bring some relief to a dispirited society. We find him repeatedly alluding to the hopelessness growing around him. In 'Vinay Patrika', he expressed grave concern about the growing social degradation, immorality, greed and sins. The tradition of the annual Ramlila continues in Varanasi. It is performed in various parts of the city.

In pursuit of his assimilating approach, Tulsidas also started organizing Krishna Lila at Tulsi Ghat. Another interesting aspect of his social engagement was the setting up of an *akhara* (a training ground for physical activities) at Tulsi Ghat. It is now used by wrestlers and bodybuilders. We know that Tulsidas had a tall and athletic personality and, probably in his youth, could have participated in such activities. An idol of Lord Hanuman, possibly placed there by Tulsidas himself, overlooks the akhara.

In Valmiki's Ramayana, Hanuman, the favourite messenger of Rama, appeared as the general-in-chief of the simian army. However, Tulsidas raised him to virtual divinity, possessing incomparable strength and deep learning. Tulsidas's Hanuman possessed both bhakti and shakti, the strength and devotion to serve his master, Lord Rama. In the Puranic tradition, Hanuman was presented as one of the eleven Rudras. But it was Tulsidas who, in Kashi's spirit of reconciliation and synthesis, firmly established Hanuman's association with Shiva. Tulsidas's Hanuman was not just a partial incarnation of Shiva. In his most popular poem, the 'Hanuman Chalisa', Tulsidas clearly described Hanuman as *Sankara Suvana*, the son of Shankara. Through his vastly popular works, Tulsidas firmly established that both of his idols, Rama and Hanuman, worshipped Shiva and acknowledged his greatness. That's how Kashi, the city of Shiva, may have influenced one of the greatest Vaishnav saints.

The idol of Hanuman at Tulsi Akhara. Tulsidas was a great devotee of Hanuman, who is a symbol of strength and energy.

The fort of Raja Chait Singh on the banks of the Ganga

The joy of bathing in the holy Ganga

Acknowledgements

This book is not my creation alone. In this seven-year-long creative journey, I have received generous backing from many friends, colleagues and family members. After working for BBC Hindi in London for over two decades, I voluntarily left it to explore new creative horizons. One of my most enjoyable projects was to launch a positive health magazine, *The Health & Happiness 4 You,* for the Indian community in the UK. A by-product of this socially enriching venture was the creation of two inspirational PowerPoint presentations. The first aimed to spread information about health among senior citizens, and the second was designed to create a mindset for positivity and success among young professionals.

When Prof. D.P. Singh, the vice chancellor of BHU, whom I have known for many years, learned about my work, he insisted that I visit his university to spread the message of positivity among his students. Regrettably, I could not make the trip while he was in office. But before he moved on to become the chairman of the University Grants Commission, he introduced me to Prof. Asha Ram Tripathi, the chairperson of the Malviya Centre for Ethics and Human Values, and Prof. Raj Kumar Singh, the dean of the Institute of Management Studies at BHU. They graciously invited me to their respective departments. The students loved my presentations. It quickly became an annual event at BHU, marking the beginning of an extraordinary fascination for Kashi, the soul of Indian civilization.

I want to express my gratitude to a dynamic government officer from India, Vishal Singh, IAS, who served as the CEO of the Kashi Vishwanath Temple Trust. He not only allowed me to film inside the temple but also suggested that if I wanted to experience the intensity and depth of Hindu faith and witness the true glory of Baba Vishwanath, I must visit the temple on its busiest day, Mahashivaratri. His successor, Dr Sunil Verma, was equally supportive and warm-heartedly supported my work during the filming of Rangbhari Ekadashi and the festival of Holi inside the renovated temple.

My special thanks to Prof. Vishwambhar Nath Mishra, the Mahant of the Sankat Mochan Hanuman Temple and the custodian of the historic Tulsi Ghat. He opened the doors of the living quarters of Saint Tulsidas and let me photograph the khadau of the poet-saint. I am also grateful to Prof. Rana P.B. Singh, formerly the professor of Cultural Landscape and Heritage Studies at BHU, for his invaluable advice and knowledge of Varanasi's history and culture. Prof. Siddharth Nath Singh, an expert in Pali and Buddhist studies, provided treasured insights into the city's life and culture. Dr B.R. Mani, renowned archaeologist and former director general of the National Museum in Delhi, offered fresh perspectives on Kashi's legacy. I had many inspiring discussions with Sanskrit scholar Lucie Guest (Divya Prabha), who left a successful investment banking career on Wall Street to live in Kashi and immerse herself in the eternal wisdom of Sanatan Dharma.

Varanasi's informal and welcoming atmosphere allowed me to forge many friendships. I can never forget the generous hospitality of Dr Divya Singh, the director of Sant Atulananda Residential Academy; the support of senior journalist from *Hindustan Times*, Amreesh Singh; filmmaker Praveen Chaturvedi; renowned classical artist and Kashi Kokila Ravati Sakalkar, and businessman friend Vaibhav Kapoor. I'm deeply indebted to my former BBC colleague, Shivkant Sharma, who unravelled the mysteries of ancient Sanskrit texts and helped me translate them accurately. I also had enlightening discussions with my friends Lalit Mohan Joshi, Kusum Joshi, Naresh Kaushik and Mira Kaushik. My colleague, Mamta Gupta, read the initial text and provided valuable suggestions.

I appreciate two PhD students from IIT BHU, Dileep Kumar Sharma and Sachin Mishra, who untiringly guided me through the city's narrow streets and numerous eateries, including the renowned Kachauri Gali.

I greatly admire the young and talented artist Sunil Kumar, whose skills and imagination allowed him to depict complex ancient stories in modern watercolour paintings.

Kashi: The Abode of Shiva would not have reached you without the gracious support of my publisher, Rupa Publications, and their team of world-class professionals. Executive Editor Yamini Chowdhury replied to my numerous queries promptly and courteously. Additionally, I'm grateful to Richa Tewari, the development editor, for providing valuable suggestions to enhance the book's flow; and Sakschi Verma, the copy editor of the book, who rigorously picked up my linguistic indiscretions.

Lastly, I must express my appreciation for three remarkable women in my life: my life partner, Renu Rana, who often had to readjust her social plans due to my long hours in the study; my daughter, Aditi Rana Khangarot, who took on the unexpected role of the family headmaster, reminding me to strictly adhere to Covid-19 protocols, such as wearing a mask and washing hands repeatedly when mingling with crowds in Varanasi; and my granddaughter, Ameya Khangarot, who had to forgo countless play sessions in the home garden with her Nana. Writing a book may be a solitary endeavour, but a successful book is never possible without the proactive support and numerous sacrifices of your family and friends.

Hanging basket lamps at Panchganga Ghat

Notes

Introduction

1. Sen, Shipli, 'Kashi Vishwanath Dham Witnesses Record 12.9 Crore Devotees in 2 Years', *India Today*, 10 December 2023, http://tinyurl.com/yh5c8tv8. Accessed on 26 December 2023.

Chapter 1: Shiva and Shakti: The Creation of Purusha and Prakriti

1. Tagare, G.V., 'Kashi Khanda, Chapter 26 – Description of Maṇikarṇikā, v: 11–17,' *The Skanda Purana*, 1950, https://bit.ly/3T6qKkJ. Accessed on 26 December 2023.
2. Tagare, G.V., 'Kashi Khanda, Chapter 26 – Description of Maṇikarṇikā, v: 24', *The Skanda Purana*, 1950, https://bit.ly/3T6qKkJ. Accessed on 3 January 2023.
3. Tagare, G.V., 'Kashi Khanda, Chapter 26 – Description of Maṇikarṇikā, v: 25–27', *The Skanda Purana*, 1950, https://bit.ly/3T6qKkJ. Accessed on 3 January 2023.
4. Tagare, G.V., 'Kashi Khanda, Chapter 99 – The Greatness of Śrī Viśveśvara, v: 4–7', *The Skanda Purana*, 1950, http://tinyurl.com/2ha3jhzw. Accessed on 26 December 2023.
5. Tagare, G.V., 'Kashi Khanda, Chapter 99 – The Greatness of Śrī Viśveśvara, v: 16–23', *The Skanda Purana*, 1950, http://tinyurl.com/2ha3jhzw. Accessed on 26 December 2023.
6. Tagare, G.V., 'Kashi Khanda, Chapter 99 – The Greatness of Śrī Viśveśvara, v: 61–2', *The Skanda Purana*, 1950, http://tinyurl.com/2ha3jhzw. Accessed on 26 December 2023.
7. Ibid.

Chapter 2 Annapurna: The Life-Giving Mother of Kashi

1. Interview with Acharya Shrikant Mishra, Pradhan Archaka of Kashi Vishwanath Temple, Varanasi, 29 November 2018.
2. Eck, Diana L., *Banaras: City of Light*, Penguin India, 1993, p. 163.
3. 'Statue from the University of Regina's Art Collection to be Returned to India Following Virtual Repatriation Ceremony', *Mackenzie Art Gallery*, 24 November 2020, https://bit.ly/419vDvb. Accessed on 11 December 2023.

Chapter 3: Gyan Vapi: Ishan Rudra digs the Wisdom Well

1. Tagare, G.V., 'Kashi Khanda, Chapter 33 – Description of Jñānavāpī, v: 12–15', *The Skanda Purana*, 1950, http://tinyurl.com/bdd6ufya. Accessed on 26 December 2023.
2. Tagare, G.V., 'Kashi Khanda, Chapter 33 – Description of Jñānavāpī, v: 1–52', *The Skanda Purana*, 1950, http://tinyurl.com/bdd6ufya. Accessed on 26 December 2023.

Chapter 4: Lingodbhav: The Genesis of the Linga of Fire

1. Shastri, J.L., 'Vidyeśvara-Saṃhitā, Chapter 1 – The Doubt of the Sages, v: 35–37', *The Shiv Purana*, 1950, https://bit.ly/3Ta7iUf. Accessed on 11 December 2023.
2. According to the Vishnu Purana, a yojana was believed to be equivalent of 12.8 km.
3. Shastri, J.L., 'Vidyeśvara-Saṃhitā, Chapter 6 – Battle Between Brahmā and Viṣṇu, v: 3–4', *The Shiv Purana*, 1950, http://tinyurl.com/2vphfbmd. Accessed on 27 December 2023.
4. Shastri, J.L., 'Vidyeśvara-Saṃhitā, Chapter 6 – Battle Between Brahmā and Viṣṇu, v: 6–7', *The Shiv Purana*, 1950, http://tinyurl.com/2vphfbmd. Accessed on 27 December 2023.
5. Shastri, J.L., 'Vidyeśvara-Saṃhitā, Chapter 7 – Śiva Manifests Himself as a Column of Fire in the Battlefield, v: 24–25', *The Shiv Purana*, 1950, http://tinyurl.com/2vphfbmd. Accessed on 27 December 2023.
6. Shastri, J.L., 'Vidyeśvara-Saṃhitā, Chapter 9 – The Proclamation of Śiva as Maheśvara (the great lord), v: 3–6', *The Shiv Purana*, http://tinyurl.com/4mc8tk7a. Accessed on 23 December 2023.
7. Shastri, J.L., 'Vidyeśvara-Saṃhitā, Chapter 9 – The Proclamation of Śiva as Maheśvara (the great lord), v: 11–14', *The Shiv Purana*, http://tinyurl.com/4mc8tk7a. Accessed on 23 December 2023.

Chapter 5: Sacred Waters: Bhagiratha And the Arrival of Ganga on Earth

1. Shastri, Hari Prasad, 'Bala Kand, Chapter 35 – The Origin of the Holy River Ganga', *Ramayana of Valmiki*, 1952, https://bit.ly/3TaC67b. Accessed on 11 December 2023.
2. Shastri, Hari Prasad, 'Bala Kand, Chapter 43 – Lord Shiva Lets Loose the Sacred River', *Ramayana of Valmiki*, 1952, https://bit.ly/3RrzLDt. Accessed on 11 December 2023.
3. Shastri, Hari Prasad, 'Bala Kand, Chapter 44 – King Bhagiratha Completes the Funeral Rites for His Ancestors', *Ramayana of Valmiki*, 1952, https://bit.ly/3t1PPm4. Accessed on 11 December 2023.

Chapter 6: The End of the Road: Moksha at Manikarnika

1. Tagare, G.V., 'Kasi Kanda, Chapter 5 – Agastya's Departure, v: 26–28', *The Skanda Purana*, 1950, http://tinyurl.com/yc7wd27c. Accessed on 27 December 2023.

2. Tagare, G.V., 'Kasi Kanda, Chapter 26 – Description of Maṇikarṇikā, v: 48–53', *The Skanda Purana*, 1950, http://tinyurl.com/yc3z4rfm. Accessed on 27 December 2023.
3. Tagare, G.V., 'Kasi Kanda, Chapter 26 – Description of Maṇikarṇikā, v: 58–69', *The Skanda Purana*, 1950, http://tinyurl.com/yc3z4rfm. Accessed on 27 December 2023.

Chapter 7: Reviving the Splendour: The Making of Kashi Vishwanath Dham

1. 'Benaras Hindu University Speech', *Bombay Sarvodaya Mandal & Gandhi Research Foundation*, http://tinyurl.com/ycj7r3u4. Accessed on 28 December 2023.
2. Eck, Diana L., *Banaras: City of Light*, Penguin, 1993, p. 82.
3. Ibid. 134.
4. Chandra, Moti, *Kashi Ka Itihasa*, Visvavidyalaya Prakashan, 1962, p. 168.
5. Ibid. 176.
6. Desai, Madhuri, *Banaras Reconstructed: Architecture and Sacred Space in a Hindu Holi City*, Orient Blackswan, India, 2017, p. 81.
7. Singh, Maharaja Sawai Man, Gopalnarayan Bahura and Chandramani Singh, *Catalogue of Historical documents in Kapad Dwara, Jaipur Part 2, Maps and Plans*, Jaipur Printers, 1990.
8. Google Earth map. Accessed on 10 December 2023.
9. Desai, Madhuri, *Banaras Reconstructed: Architecture and Sacred Space in a Hindu Holi City*, Orient Blackswan, India, 2017, p. 82.
10. Eck, Diana L., *Banaras: City of Light*, Penguin, 1993, p. 135.
11. Interview with Prof. Rana P.B. Singh, professor of Cultural Geography and Heritage Studies, Banaras Hindu University, Varanasi, 19 January 2019.

Chapter 10: Tulsidas: Assimilating Rama and Shiva

1. Tulsidas, 'Lanka Khanda', *Ramcharitamanas*, Gita Press, Gorakhpur, p. 827.
2. Tulsidas, 'Uttara Khanda', *Ramcharitamanas*, Gita Press, Gorakhpur, p. 1081.
3. Interview with Mahant Vishwambhar Nath Mishra at Tulsi Ghat, Varanasi, 13 March 2022.